FRENCH RIVIERA
Travel Guide
2023

PROF. LUCY STONE

Copyright © Prof. Lucy Stone, 2023.

All rights reserved. No part of this publication may be reproduced, distributed or transmitted in any form or by any means, including photocopying, recording, or other electronic or mechanical methods, without the prior written permission of the publisher, except in the case of brief quotations embodied in critical reviews and certain other noncommercial uses permitted by copyright law.

TABLE OF CONTENTS

INTRODUCTION 7

    My Exciting Moments In French Riviera 7

    A Glimpse of Paradise 8

    What you need to know before you go 8

    Reasons To Explore The French Riviera 11

TRAVEL ADVICE 16

    Navigating the Region 16

    Language and Communication Tips 16

    Currency and Payment Methods 18

SAFETY AND HEALTH 20

    Safety Considerations 20

    Health Considerations 21

PACKING ESSENTIALS FOR THE FRENCH RIVIERA
.... 23

BUDGETING TIPS 26

BEST TIME TO VISIT 29

    Seasons at the Riviera 29

ENTRY REQUIREMENTS AND DOCUMENTATION 32

HIDDEN GEMS OFF THE TOURIST PART 36

    Top Places to Visit 37

OUTDOOR ACTIVITIES 43

NIGHT AMUSEMENTS AND ENTERTAINMENT 45

    Cultural Events 46

FOODS 47

    Seafood Extravaganza 47

    Wine and Tastings 47

    Local Markets and Gourmet Shops 48

SHOPPING SPREE 49

    Fashion Boutiques 49

    Artisanal Markets 49

    Antique Treasures 50

PRACTICAL TIPS FOR A SMOOTH VISIT 52

    Local Etiquette 52

    Tipping Customs 53

    Sustainable Travel Practices 53

DAY TRIPS & EXCURSIONS 55

   Discovering Nearby Towns 55

   Scenic Drives around the Coast 56

BONUS 57

   French Riviera Phrases And Their Meanings 57

   4 Days Itinerary 60

CONCLUSION 63

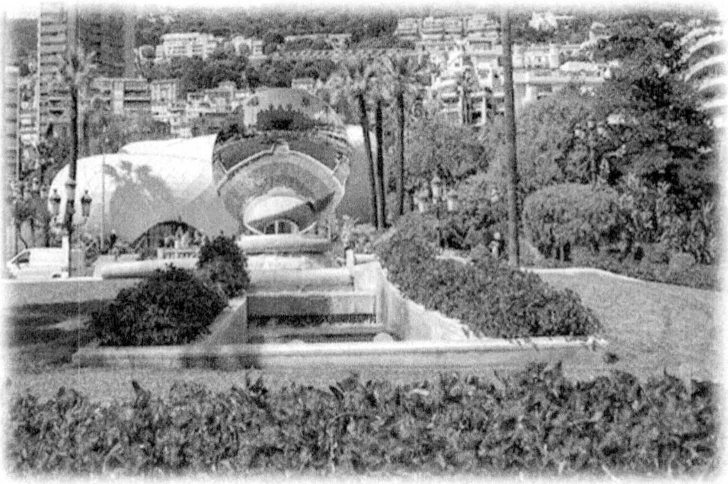

INTRODUCTION

My Exciting Moments In French Riviera

Have you ever felt the Mediterranean sun warm your skin as you walked down the Promenade des Anglais in Nice? Or maybe you've marveled at the ageless beauty of Eze? Maybe you've danced the night away in Monaco's famous casinos or soaked in the allure of St. Tropez's gorgeous streets.

If these encounters seem like faraway dreams, let me assure you, they need not stay such. The French Riviera, with its sundrenched beaches, rich cultural history, and spectacular nightlife, is not a world of dreams; it's a place eager to welcome you.

My name is Prof. Lucy Stone, and I've been lucky enough to find the hidden jewels and famous monuments of the French Riviera. Now, I want to share my enthusiasm and expertise with you via this complete manual.

With those pages, you'll uncover the secrets to traversing this interesting location. I'll bring you to the sun soaked beaches, art and culture aplenty, gastronomic pleasures, and spectacular nightlife that make the French Riviera an unrivaled destination.

But this isn't simply a guide; it's an encouragement to begin on your own trip. As you immerse yourself in the tales and thoughts provided here, the Riviera will lure you closer. The magnetism of the Mediterranean will tug at your emotions, tempting you to experience its charm firsthand.

A Glimpse of Paradise

What you need to know before you go

As you set foot on the French Riviera, you'll quickly feel like you've reached a paradise on Earth. This famed stretch of shoreline, also known as the Côte d'Azur, is a mesmerizing combination of natural beauty and human artistry. The instant you arrive, you're met with blue oceans, palm lined boulevards, and a seemingly limitless supply of sunlight.

- ❖ Beaches: One of the most outstanding aspects of the French Riviera is its gorgeous beaches. If you choose to rest on the pebbly beaches of Nice, the sandy stretches of Cannes, or the secret coves of Antibes, you'll find yourself in coastal paradise.
- ❖ Crystal clear seas softly lap the shore, beckoning you for a refreshing swim or a relaxing sunbath.
- ❖ Picturesque Towns: Along the shoreline, you'll discover a number of attractive towns and cities, each with its own distinct character.
- ❖ Nice, with its famed Promenade des Anglais, emanates an aura of refinement. Antibes, with its antique fortifications and cobblestone alleyways, gives a look into history. Then there's

the gorgeous Monaco, where elegance and grandeur are on full display.

❖ Majestic Landscapes: Venture a bit inland, and you'll encounter stunning natural vistas. The undulating hills of Provence are covered with vineyards and lavender farms, providing a painter's pallet of hues and smells. The Alpes Maritimes provide hiking routes that lead to awe inspiring vistas, enabling you to drink in the splendor of the Mediterranean from above.

❖ Rich Cultural Heritage: Beyond its natural beauty, the French Riviera features a rich cultural past that has captivated painters, poets, and philosophers for ages.

❖ Art and Museums: The area has been a muse to innumerable painters, notably Marc Chagall and Henri Matisse, who found inspiration in its light and scenery.

❖ The Matisse Museum in Nice and the Picasso Museum in Antibes feature their works. You may also tour the Fondation Maeght in Saint Paul de Vence, an architectural masterpiece that contains an extraordinary collection of modern and contemporary art.

❖ Historical Sites: The French Riviera is rich in history. Visit the old Roman remains at Cimiez, where you may explore the remnants of a Roman city and an outstanding amphitheater.

- Antibes' ancient town is ringed by 16thcentury walls, while the Palace of the Princes in Monaco is a testimony to the region's royal heritage.

- Festivals & Events: Throughout the year, the French Riviera comes alive with festivals honoring music, movies, and more. The Cannes Film Festival draws A list superstars, while the Nice Jazz Festival provides a broad roster of musical talents. Be sure to check the local event schedule during your stay.

- The Allure of the Mediterranean: The Mediterranean Sea is the heart and soul of the French Riviera, and its fascination is irresistible.

- Mediterranean Cuisine: The region's culinary landscape is greatly affected by its closeness to the sea. Indulge in fresh seafood, and juicy Provencal dishes like ratatouille, and appreciate the simplicity of a Mediterranean diet rich in olive oil and colorful greens. Dining at a beachside restaurant as the sun sets over the ocean is an experience you won't forget.

- Water Activities: The Mediterranean provides a paradise for water aficionados. You may go sailing in the deep blue seas, snorkeling to investigate marine life, or even try your hand at water sports like jet skiing and paddle boarding.
- The quiet, pleasant seas make it excellent for both novices and expert water enthusiasts.

- ❖ Relaxation and Wellness: The Mediterranean environment is recognized for its therapeutic benefits. Many travelers come to the French Riviera seeking leisure and renewal.
- ❖ You'll discover various spas and wellness facilities that provide massages, yoga, and other wellness treatments to help you rest and recharge.

Reasons To Explore The French Riviera

Sun Drenched Beaches

The French Riviera is renowned for sundrenched beaches that match the greatest in the world. With almost 300 days of sunlight a year, this Mediterranean paradise provides an excellent atmosphere for beach enthusiasts.

The beaches here are varied, catering to various preferences. From the pebbly coastlines of Nice, where the turquoise seas create a stark contrast, to the golden sands of Antibes and Cannes, each beach provides a distinct experience.

Water Sports Extravaganza: If you're an adventure seeker, the Riviera won't disappoint. From jet skiing to parasailing, there's a vast selection of water activities to pick from. Crystal clear waters make snorkeling and scuba diving a thrill, displaying a lively undersea world with marine life.

Beach Clubs and Luxe Lounging: The Riviera is recognized for its beautiful beach clubs that give the ultimate of coastal luxury.
With soft loungers, attentive service, and magnificent vistas, these clubs are popular among the jetset crowd.

Drink a cool glass of rosé at Nikki Beach in Cannes or enjoy a private cabana at Larvotto Beach in Monaco, the experience is nothing short of spectacular.

Art & Culture Galore

The French Riviera has always been a fascination for artists, authors, and creative minds seeking inspiration from its ethereal vistas and bright light.

- Museums and Galleries: The area is home to an excellent collection of museums and galleries. The Marc Chagall National Museum in Nice has the greatest public collection of his paintings.

- The Fondation Maeght at Saint Paul de Vence is a masterpiece itself, nestled within beautiful grounds and presenting a broad collection of modern and contemporary art.

- Historical Enclaves: Beyond art, the Riviera possesses a rich historical tapestry. The historic town of Antibes, encircled by 16thcentury fortifications, takes you back in time.

- Explore the Roman remains at Cimiez, including an amphitheater that tells of old gladiatorial games. Monaco's Prince's Palace, positioned high on the Rock, looks at the principality's royal heritage.

Food

The French Riviera is a gourmet wonderland, with its cuisine reflecting the sunsoaked aromas of the Mediterranean.

- ➢ **Provençal Delights:** The food here is defined by the use of fresh, local ingredients. Ratatouille, a dish of stewed vegetables, epitomizes the simplicity and flavors of Provencal cookery. Olive oil, herbs, and fragrant spices enrich every meal, providing a sensual treat.

- ➢ **Seafood Extravaganza:** Given its seaside position, the Riviera is a seafood lover's dream. From luscious bouillabaisse in Marseille to oysters from the Thau Lagoon, you'll discover an assortment of coastal delights. Pair these meals with a local rosé or crisp white wine for a real sense of the area.

- ➢ **Market Wonders:** Explore the lively marketplaces that dot the Riviera. The Cours Saleya Market in Nice is a sensory explosion, with booths bursting with fresh food, flowers, and local specialties. Pick grab a baguette, some cheese, and olives for a picnic by the water.

Glamorous Nightlife

As the sun sets over the Mediterranean, the French Riviera changes into a paradise for night owls and party fanatics.

- ➢ **Chic Bars & Lounges:** From the glamorous bars of Cannes to the stylish beach clubs of SaintTropez, the nightlife here radiates elegance. Sip on freshly made cocktails while taking in magnificent views of the shore. The Casino Square in Monte Carlo, Monaco, provides a magnificent environment for visitors wishing to try their luck.

- ➢ Nightclubs for Every Taste: The Riviera's nightlife culture caters to a broad audience. You may dance the night away at iconic clubs like Jimmy'z in Monaco or enjoy live music in quieter places in Nice's Old Town.You like electronic rhythms or live jazz, you'll find a location that meets your musical taste.

TRAVEL ADVICE

Navigating the Region

The French Riviera, often known as the Côte d'Azur, covers over 550 miles of coastline, comprising a myriad of towns, cities, and lovely villages. Navigating this area effectively and appreciating everything it has to offer takes a planned approach.

Useful applications and Guides: Smartphone applications like Google Maps and transit apps relevant to the area may be essential for traveling. Additionally, consider having a hardcopy guidebook or map for places with minimal connection.

Language and Communication Tips

- While French is the official language of the French Riviera, you'll discover that English is often used in tourist areas. However, making an effort to speak a few simple French words may go a long way in enriching your trip.

- Basic words: Learning a few essential words like greetings, "thank you" (merci), "please" (s'il vous plaît), and "excuse me" (excusezmoi) may be extremely beneficial. Locals enjoy it when tourists attempt to speak their language.

- English in Tourist Areas: In renowned tourist sites like Nice, Cannes, and Monaco, you'll find numerous individuals who are proficient in English. Hotels, restaurants, and stores in these locations commonly have English speaking employees.

- Local Dialects: In certain regions, especially smaller villages, you could find local dialects like Nicois in Nice. While not essential for basic conversation, it may be an interesting cultural experience to learn a few phrases or expressions.

- Politeness and Etiquette: Politeness is highly prized in French society. Using formal pleasantries like "Bonjour" (good morning) and "Bonsoir" (good evening) is traditional. Remember to say "s'il vous plaît" (please) and "merci" (thank you) when appropriate.

- NonVerbal Communication: Pay attention to nonverbal signs including body language and facial expressions. These may give significant background to interactions.

- Phrasebook or Language App: Carrying a phrasebook or utilizing a language app on your phone may be immensely handy, particularly in more distant locations where English might not be as often spoken.

Currency and Payment Methods

The official currency of France, including the French Riviera, is the Euro (€).

- ❖ Cash Usage: While credit and debit cards are generally accepted, it's good to carry some cash for minor transactions, markets, and businesses that may not take cards. ATMs (distributeur automatique) are frequently accessible in towns and cities.

- ❖ Credit and Debit Cards: Major credit and debit cards (Visa, MasterCard, American Express) are frequently accepted at hotels, restaurants, stores, and other venues. It's a good idea to advise your bank of your trip intentions to prevent any complications with card use.

- ❖ Contactless Payments: Contactless payment solutions like Apple Pay and Google Pay are becoming more popular and generally accepted.

- ❖ Traveler's Checks: While traveler's checks used to be a frequent method of payment for overseas travelers, they are less widely utilized now. It's more practical to depend on a mix of cash and cards.

- ❖ Tipping Customs: Tipping is traditional in France but not mandatory. In restaurants, it's traditional to give a modest tip (typically about 10%) if service is not included. In cafés, rounding up the tab or leaving some change is welcomed.

- ❖ Tax-Free Shopping: If you're a non-EU resident, you may be entitled to tax rebates on some purchases. Look for stores displaying a "Tax-Free Shopping" sign and ask for a tax refund form while making qualified purchases.

SAFETY AND HEALTH

Safety Considerations

General Safety

Low Crime Rates: The French Riviera usually has low crime rates, making it a safe location. However, as with any tourist site, minor theft may occur. Keep a watch on your possessions, particularly in busy locations.

Traffic Safety: Be careful while crossing streets, since traffic might be hectic. Use marked crosswalks and obey traffic signals.

Emergency Numbers: The emergency number in France is 112, which links you to police, fire, and medical services.

Natural Safety

Beach Safety: Follow any posted warnings or flags on beaches. Pay heed to lifeguard directions, particularly if there are strong currents or rough waves.

Trekking Safety: If you intend on trekking in the local hills or mountains, please be sure to use established paths and be equipped with adequate footwear and equipment.

Health Considerations

Travel Insurance

It's definitely suggested to get travel insurance that covers medical expenditures. This might be essential in case of unforeseen sickness or accidents.

Vaccinations and Health Precautions:

Check with your doctor before flying to verify you're up-to-date on regular vaccines. Depending on your trip intentions, you may require extra immunizations or measures.

Sun Protection:
The Mediterranean sun may be fierce. Wear sunscreen, sunglasses, and a hat, and seek shade during high solar hours.

Water Safety:
Tap water is typically safe to drink in most locations of the French Riviera. However, if you're uncertain, it's preferable to consume bottled water.

Medical Facilities

High-quality medical treatment is widely accessible on the French Riviera. Larger cities like Nice and Cannes offer outstanding hospitals and medical facilities.

Pharmacies:

Pharmacies are prevalent and may supply over-the-counter and prescription drugs. They also give guidance on minor health conditions.

Food Safety

The cuisine on the French Riviera is typically safe to eat. However, if you have special dietary requirements or allergies, explain this openly while eating out.

Insect Precautions:

During the summer, there might be mosquitoes. Consider packing bug repellent and wearing long sleeves in the evenings.

PACKING ESSENTIALS FOR THE FRENCH RIVIERA

Clothing

- ❖ Light and Breathable Fabrics: Given the warm Mediterranean climate, pack lightweight, breathable fabrics like cotton and linen. These will keep you comfortable in the summer heat.

- ❖ Swimwear: If you're lounging on the beach, taking a dip in the Mediterranean, make sure to pack your favorite swimsuits.

- ❖ Sun Protection: A wide brimmed hat, sunglasses, and high-SPF sunscreen for protecting yourself from the strong sun.

- ❖ Casual and Semi-Formal Wear: While the French Riviera is generally relaxed, it's a good idea to have some slightly dressier options for dining out in the evenings.

- ❖ Comfortable Shoes: Comfortable walking shoes are essential, especially if you plan on exploring charming old towns or going on nature hikes.

- ❖ Light Jacket or Sweater: Even in the summer, evenings can be cooler, so it's wise to have a light jacket or sweater for added warmth.

Travel Accessories

7. Travel Adapter: France uses Type C and E plugs, so make sure you have the appropriate adapter for your devices.

8. Portable Charger: Keep your devices charged while you're out exploring. Especially if you're using your phone for navigation.

9. Travel Pillow and Blanket: If you're taking a long flight or train ride, having a comfortable pillow and blanket can make the journey much more pleasant.

10. Reusable Water Bottle: Staying hydrated is important, especially in the summer heat. Having a reusable water bottle will help you save money and reduce plastic waste.

11. Daypack or Tote Bag: A small daypack or tote bag is useful for carrying essentials like water, sunscreen, and your camera while you're out exploring.

12. Documents and Copies: Don't forget your passport, visa (if required), travel insurance documents, and any necessary reservations. It's also a good idea to have photocopies or digital copies stored in a secure location.

Toiletries and Personal Items

13. Toiletry Bag: Pack your essential toiletries, including toothbrush, toothpaste, shampoo,

conditioner, soap, and any other personal items you may need.

14. Medications: If you have any prescription medications, be sure to bring an ample supply and carry them in their original containers.

15. First Aid Kit: Include basic items like band-aids, antiseptic cream, pain relievers, and any specific medications you may need.

16. Cosmetics and Grooming Products: Bring your makeup, skincare products, and grooming essentials.

Entertainment and Miscellaneous:

17. Books or E-Reader: If you enjoy reading, having a book or e-reader can be a great way to relax during downtime.

18. Travel Journal: Documenting your experiences can be a wonderful way to remember your trip. Bring a journal or use a notetaking app on your phone.

19. Camera and Accessories: Capture the beauty of the French Riviera with your camera or smartphone. Don't forget extra memory cards and chargers.

20. Snacks: Having some snacks on hand can be a lifesaver, especially if you're on a long journey or exploring remote areas.

BUDGETING TIPS

1. Set a Realistic Budget

Determine how much you're willing to spend overall and assign precise amounts for individual categories like hotel, meals, transportation, activities, and mementos.

2. Travel During Off-Peak Seasons

Consider coming during shoulder seasons (spring or autumn) when rates for lodging and activities tend to be cheaper, and crowds are lighter.

3. Accommodation Choices

Look for budget-friendly housing choices such as hostels, guesthouses, or vacation rentals. You might also try vacationing in less tourist regions for lower costs.

4. Use Public Transportation

Utilize the efficient and cost-effective public transit system. Trains and buses are fantastic methods to move about the French Riviera without breaking the bank.

5. Eat Like a Local

Opt for smaller, local eateries and markets rather than tourist heavy establishments. This not only gives a genuine experience but is frequently more budget friendly.

6. Cook or Picnic

If you have access to a kitchen (particularly in vacation rentals), try making some of your meals. Additionally, picnics in parks or along the beach may be a fun and cost effective eating alternative.

7. Free and Low Cost Activities

Take advantage of the numerous free or low cost activities available, such as touring historical towns, hiking, visiting public beaches, or attending local festivals and events.

8. Avoid Tourist Traps

Be careful of tourist heavy regions where costs may be exaggerated. Instead, seek for less crowded, more real encounters.

9. Discounts and Passes

Look for city or regional passes that give savings on transit, museums, and attractions. These may yield considerable discounts, particularly if you intend to visit many places.

10. Limit Extravagant Spending

While it's tempting to indulge in luxury experiences, consider placing a limit on more costly activities like high end eating or pricey trips.

11. Plan and Book in Advance

Booking transportation, housing, and some activities ahead of time may frequently lead to better bargains and save last minute, possibly pricey selections.

12. Monitor Expenses

Keep track of your expenditures during the vacation to ensure you remain within your budget. There are several budgeting applications available to aid you with this.

13. Flexible Itinerary

Leave space for spontaneity. Being open to adjusting plans based on local advice or unforeseen possibilities might lead to unique and budget friendly experiences.

14. Avoid Unnecessary Fees

Be careful of ATM fees, international transaction fees, and other unexpected expenses. Consider selecting a bank or credit card that provides advantageous conditions for overseas travel.

BEST TIME TO VISIT

Seasons at the Riviera

1. Spring (March to May):

Spring is a great time to visit the French Riviera. The weather begins to warm up, and the landscapes explode into brilliant hues as flowers blossom.

Advantages: Mild temps (avg. 15 20°C / 59 68°F) Fewer people compared to the summer months Ideal for outdoor activities like hiking and cycling
Perfect for exploring gardens and parks

Ideal Activities: Visit the famed gardens in Nice
Explore the historic towns of Antibes and Villefranchesur Mer.
Enjoy picnics on the beach or in parks.

2. Summer (June to August):

Summer is the main tourist season on the French Riviera, and with good reason. The Mediterranean climate is at its peak, bringing lengthy days of sunlight.

Advantages: Warm to hot conditions (avg. 25 30°C / 77 86°F) Vibrant environment with various events and festivals
Ideal for beach activities and water sports Perfect for stylish nightlife and eating

Ideal Activities: Sunbathe and swim at the gorgeous beaches of Nice, Cannes, and Saint Tropez.
Attend the Cannes Film Festival or Monaco Grand Prix (if traveling in May).
Experience the bustling nightlife in locales like Nice's Old Town or Monaco's casinos.

3. Autumn (September to November):

Autumn delivers a smooth shift from the summer heat to colder weather. The throngs start to thin away, providing for a more comfortable encounter.

Advantages: Pleasant temps (avg. 18 23°C / 64 73°F) Harvest season with local culinary festivals and wine events Ideal for touring vineyards and wineries in the region
Comfortable for activities like hiking or sightseeing

Ideal Activities: Visit vineyards and sample local wines in locations like Provence and Var.
Explore the colorful marketplaces in locations like Nice and Antibes.
Go hiking in the Esterel Mountains for spectacular fall vistas.

4. Winter (December to February):

While the winter months are colder, the French Riviera has a comparatively pleasant temperature compared to other regions of Europe. It's a pleasant time to visit.

Advantages: Mild temps (avg. 10 15°C / 50 59°F)
Lower lodging rates and fewer visitors

Ideal for cultural and historical explorations Perfect for cozying up in cafés and savoring local food

Ideal Activities: Visit museums and historical places like the Picasso Museum in Antibes.
Explore the lovely Christmas markets in places like Nice and Cannes.
Enjoy winter activities in the neighboring Alps.

Ideal Months for Different Activities

Beach and Water Activities: Best Time: June to September The Mediterranean Sea is hottest during these months, making it great for swimming, snorkeling, and other water activities.

Hiking and Outdoor Adventures: Best Time: April to June, September to October Mild weather and flowering landscapes make spring and early autumn great for trekking and outdoor activities.

Cultural and Historical Explorations: Best Time: Anytime The French Riviera's rich cultural legacy may be experienced year round. Museums, historical landmarks, and attractive ancient towns are constantly accessible.

Wine Tasting and Culinary Experiences: Best Time: September to November The grape harvest season gives a fantastic chance for wine sampling and savoring the local cuisine.

ENTRY REQUIREMENTS AND DOCUMENTATION

Visa Requirements:

EU/EEA Citizens: If you are a citizen of a European Union (EU) or European Economic Area (EEA) nation, you do not require a visa to visit France, including the French Riviera. You may remain for an indefinite duration as long as you have a valid ID card or passport.

Non-EU/EEA nationals: Non-EU/EEA nationals may need a Schengen visa to access the French Riviera. The Schengen visa permits you to remain in France and the Schengen Area for up to 90 days within a 180day period for tourist, business, or family trips.

Visa Application Process:

1. Check Visa Requirements: Verify whether you require a visa to visit France on the official website of the French government or contact the closest French consulate or embassy.

2. Apply in Advance: If a visa is necessary, apply well in advance of your anticipated trip dates. Processing timeframes may vary based on your country of residency.

3. Gather Required Documents: Passport with at least two blank pages and valid for at least three months

beyond your scheduled departure from the Schengen Area.
   Completed visa application form.
   Passport-sized photographs.
   Proof of lodging and travel itinerary.
   Proof of adequate finances for the length of your stay.
   Travel insurance with coverage of at least €30,000 for medical costs and repatriation.

4. Organize an Appointment: Contact the closest French consulate or embassy to organize a visa appointment.

5. Attend the Interview: Attend the visa interview at the consulate or embassy. Be prepared to give biometric data, if requested.

6. Pay the Visa charge: Pay the relevant visa charge, which varies based on your nationality and visa type.

7. Wait for Processing: Wait for the visa to be processed. Processing periods might vary from a few days to many weeks.

8. Obtain Your Visa: Once accepted, you will obtain a visa sticker on your passport. Verify the information to confirm they are right.

Passport Validity

  EU/EEA nationals: EU and EEA nationals require a valid ID card or passport to enter France.

Non-EU/EEA nationals: Non-EU/EEA nationals must have a passport that is valid for at least three months after their anticipated departure from the Schengen Area.

Travelers with Residency: If you are a resident of a Schengen nation, your passport should be valid for at least three months beyond your anticipated departure from the Schengen Area.

It's necessary to examine the precise entrance criteria for your nationality before visiting.

Travel Insurance

Requirement: It is strongly suggested to have travel insurance that covers medical expenditures, including emergency and repatriation, with a minimum coverage of €30,000. Some nations may need evidence of travel insurance for visa applications.

Coverage: In addition to medical coverage, consider insurance that also covers trip cancellation, lost or delayed baggage, and other unexpected occurrences.

Obtain in Advance: It's essential to obtain travel insurance before your trip. Review various policies to ensure they match your individual requirements.

Verify Coverage: Read the policy carefully to understand what is covered and how to lodge a claim in case of emergency.

7.

Best Attractions in the French Riviera

Iconic Landmarks and Monuments

1. Promenade des Anglais (Nice): This landmark promenade along the Bay of Angels in Nice is recognized for its breathtaking coastal vistas, palmlined boulevard, and energetic atmosphere. It's a fantastic area for a leisurely walk or to relax on the beach.

2. Palais des Festivals et des Congrès (Cannes): The Palais des Festivals is a hallmark of Cannes' worldwide film festival reputation. This remarkable edifice holds diverse events and is situated on the renowned La Croisette promenade.

3. Prince's Palace of Monaco (MonacoVille): Overlooking the Mediterranean, this medieval house is the official home of the Prince of Monaco. Visitors may tour its luxurious state suites and enjoy panoramic views of the city.

4. home Ephrussi de Rothschild (Saint-Jean-Cap-Ferrat): This Belle Époque home is surrounded by gorgeous themed gardens, each with its distinct charm. The villa's art collection and the vistas of the French Riviera make it a must visit.

5. Old Town (Vieux Nice): The Old Town of Nice is a tangle of small alleyways, colorful houses, and lively marketplaces.

HIDDEN GEMS OFF THE TOURIST PART

1. Eze Village: Perched on a hill, Eze Village provides medieval charm and beautiful vistas. Wander through its charming alleys, see the Jardin Exotique with unusual cactus, and explore the art galleries.

2. Île Sainte-Marguerite (Cannes): Escape to this quiet island right off Cannes' shore. It's home to beautiful woods, isolated beaches, and the ancient Fort Royal, famed for the Man in the Iron Mask tale.

3. Roquebrune-Cap-Martin: Nestled between Monaco and Menton, this hamlet has a historic village with small alleyways and breathtaking views from the Roquebrune Cap Martin Promenade.

4. Villa Kérylos (BeaulieusurMer): Experience ancient Greek luxury in this painstakingly reconstructed house. It's a hidden jewel that gives a unique view into Hellenistic architecture and society.

5. Chapelle de SaintPierre des Pêcheurs (Villefranchesur Mer): Also known as the Fishermen's church, this modest church near the sea is filled with bright murals representing marine life. It's a calm and creative getaway.

8. Absolutely, let's go further into each of these fantastic destinations:

Top Places to Visit

1. Promenade des Anglais (Nice)

Mediterranean, the Promenade des Anglais in Nice serves as an archetypal symbol of the French Riviera's elegance and beauty. Stretching for roughly seven kilometers, this renowned promenade gives a panoramic view of the Baie des Anges, enticing tourists with its serene water and bustling ambiance.

Lined with gigantic palm trees and accented with inviting azure seats, it gives the ideal backdrop for a leisurely walk, a refreshing jog, or just soaking in the warmth of the Riviera sun.

In the early morning, the promenade comes alive with residents running down the seashore, but as the day develops, it morphs into a kaleidoscope of activity. Street entertainers, artisans, and sellers provide an artistic flavor, enabling you to immerse yourself in the local culture.

For those seeking leisure, the Promenade des Anglais provides various locations to stretch out on the pebbled beach, letting the waves serenade you into a state of peaceful calm. This legendary stretch of shoreline captures the very core of the Riviera's attraction, flawlessly merging natural beauty with an aura of elegant leisure.

2. Old Town of Antibes

Stepping into the Old Town of Antibes is like entering a time capsule of Provençal history and charm. Enclosed by centurie sold stone walls, this tiny area takes tourists back to a period of small cobblestone alleys, pastelhued houses, and a real feeling of history.

Meandering through the labyrinthine lanes, you'll uncover artisan stores, pleasant cafés, and art galleries showing the skills of both local and international artists.

The Picasso Museum, situated in the ancient Château Grimaldi, gives a stunning view into the creative mind of the great artist, who spent a substantial chunk of his life in Antibes. As you visit the museum's halls, you'll see an assortment of Picasso's works, each carrying the imprint of his particular style and ingenuity.

Beyond the artistic treasures, the Old Town is also home to the colorful Provençal Market, a sensory treat where the aroma of fresh herbs mingles with the rich colors of local products and the boisterous conversation of merchants.

3. Monaco's Glittering Allure

The Principality of Monaco calls with an attraction that is nothing short of spectacular. Synonymous with grandeur, elegance, and wealth, Monaco is a place that epitomizes the very essence of the Riviera's refinement. The world renowned Casino de Monte-

Carlo stands as a tribute to the grandeur that Monaco exudes, where the chandeliers glimmer with sumptuous brightness, and the roulette wheels spin with an air of expectation.

A vacation to Monaco wouldn't be complete without a walk through the pristine grounds of Jardin Exotique. Perched high above the Mediterranean, these gardens provide a stunning perspective of the Riviera coastline, highlighted by an assortment of unique succulents and cacti from across the globe.
For a sense of regality, watch the Changing of the Guard at the Prince's Palace, an event that emanates tradition and grandeur.

As the sun sets, the lights of Monaco begin to glimmer, throwing an alluring radiance over the citystate. From the Rock of Monaco, the vista stretches across the port, producing a sight that is nothing short of breathtaking. This mix of elegance, history, and natural beauty makes Monaco a spectacular diamond on the crown of the French Riviera.

Cannes: Beyond the Film Festival

While Cannes is mainly linked with its lavish film festival, there's much more to this gorgeous city on the French Riviera. Beyond the red carpets and celebrity sightings, Cannes presents a rich trove of cultural, gastronomic, and natural pleasures.

- ❖ Cultural Riches: Take a walk through the lovely Old Town, known as Le Suquet, with its cobblestone streets and antique buildings. Visit the Museé de la Castre, nestled in a medieval castle, to discover an outstanding collection of Mediterranean art and antiques. Don't miss the tranquil Chapelle de la Miséricorde, a wonderful specimen of Baroque architecture.

- ❖ Beachfront Bliss: Cannes features some of the Riviera's most renowned beaches. Plage de la Croisette is noted for its golden beaches and crystal clear seas. You may also unwind at one of the exclusive beach clubs, where you can enjoy sunbeds and exquisite food.

- ❖ Shopping and Dining: Rue d'Antibes is a heaven for shopping, packed with luxury stores and stylish businesses. After a day of shopping therapy, sample the local food at one of Cannes' great restaurants. Fresh seafood, Provençal meals, and scrumptious pastries await your taste buds.

- ❖ Iles de Lérins: A short boat journey from Cannes, the Iles de Lérins provide a calm respite. Explore the ancient Fort Royal on Île Sainte-Marguerite, noted for sheltering the enigmatic Man in the Iron Mask. On Île Saint-Honorat, explore the Cistercian abbey and enjoy the quiet environment.

Cannes, despite its film festival glamor, is a diverse resort that flawlessly integrates culture, leisure, and natural beauty.

St. Tropez

St. Tropez, with its blue seas and famed nightlife, has long been the playground of the affluent and famous. This Mediterranean treasure provides far more than its flashy image indicates.

- ❖ scenic Port: The scenic Old Port, or Vieux Port, is a hive of activity. Watch colorful fishing boats swing softly over the sea while having a café au lait at a waterside café. Stroll around the quays and visit the local shops and galleries.

- ❖ Beaches: St. Tropez is surrounded by gorgeous beaches, each with its distinct character. Pampelonne Beach is noted for its golden beaches and beach clubs, while Plage de la Ponche provides a calmer, more personal atmosphere. Water sports aficionados will find lots of alternatives along the shore.

- ❖ Art and Culture: Discover the artistic side of St. Tropez at the Musée de l'Annonciade, home to an excellent collection of Impressionist and post Impressionist artworks. The town has always been a sanctuary for artists, and you'll find galleries showing current artwork throughout the streets.

- ❖ Town Charm: Beyond the glamour of the harbor, enjoy the quaint alleyways of the town. Stroll through winding alleyways, uncover secret squares, and appreciate the pastel-hued cottages decked with bright flowers. Place des

Lices features a busy market where residents and tourists congregate to purchase fresh fruit and Provençal delights.

- ❖ Nightlife: St. Tropez's nightlife is famed. From world renowned nightclubs to small pubs, there's something for everyone. Dance the night away or have a calm beverage overlooking the port.

OUTDOOR ACTIVITIES

Water Sports and Beaches

1. Water activities: The French Riviera's crystal clear seas are great for a multitude of water activities, including snorkeling, scuba diving, windsurfing, and paddle boarding. The Mediterranean Sea offers perfect circumstances for both novices and seasoned lovers.

2. Beaches: The Riviera features some of the world's most renowned beaches. If you like the fashionable beach clubs of Pampe-lonne in St. Tropez, the pebbled coastline of Nice, the hidden coves of Cap d'Antibes, you'll find a beach to fit your taste.

Hiking and Nature Trails

3. Hiking: The French Riviera provides a diversified scenery for hikers. Explore the Alpes Maritimes and the Parc National du Mercantour, where you may go on routes that lead to stunning mountain panoramas and calm alpine lakes.

4. Coastal Walks: Discover magnificent coastal routes such as the Cap Ferrat coastal trail. These routes give spectacular views of the Mediterranean, leading you past thick foliage and secret coves.

Golfing

5. Golf Courses: Golf fans will be pleased by the various world class golf courses around the French Riviera. Try

the Royal Mougins Golf Club or the Monte Carlo Golf Club, both providing demanding courses with magnificent vistas.

Cycling Routes with Scenic Views

6. Cycling: The French Riviera is a sanctuary for bikers. Ride along lovely seaside routes or push yourself with mountain ascents in the Alpes Maritimes. The Col de l'Èze and Col de Turini are notable hills among cyclists.

7. Bike lanes: For a more peaceful riding experience, consider dedicated bike lanes like the Promenade des Anglais in Nice, which provides spectacular coastal vistas without the need to fight with traffic.

NIGHT AMUSEMENTS AND ENTERTAINMENT

Chic Bars and Lounges

1. Le Negresco Bar (Nice):   In the renowned Negresco Hotel, this bar oozes old world charm and elegance. Enjoy a handpicked range of drinks in a refined environment with magnificent views of the Mediterranean.

2. La Guérite (Cannes):   Located on the calm Île Sainte Marguerite, La Guérite provides a unique combination of seaside leisure and stylish nightlife. Sip cocktails while basking in the sea wind and the breathtaking views of Cannes.

3. Blue Gin Bar (Monaco):   Situated in the legendary Monte Carlo Bay Hotel, the Blue Gin Bar provides a modern ambiance with a range of distinctive drinks. The patio facing the sea is great for a quiet evening.

Nightclubs for Every Taste

4. VIP Room (Saint-Tropez):   A cornerstone of Saint-Tropez nightlife, the VIP Room is linked with elegance and Alist celebrity sightings. Expect intense music and a vibrant audience dancing the night away.

5. Jimmy'z (Monaco):   This iconic nightclub in the heart of MonteCarlo is recognized for its dynamic atmosphere and worldclass DJs. The openair patio offers a wonderful setting for an amazing night.

6. Les Caves du Roy (Saint-Tropez): Located in the renowned Hotel Byblos, Les Caves du Roy is a must visit for visitors seeking a spectacular nightlife experience. The club's luxurious décor and high energy sounds make it a favorite for foreign jetsetters.

Cultural Events

7. Nice Jazz Festival (Nice): Held annually in July, the Nice Jazz Festival is one of the oldest and most recognized jazz events in the world. Enjoy performances by world class musicians against the background of the Mediterranean.

8. Cannes Film Festival (Cannes): If you manage to come in May, the Cannes Film Festival is an unequaled cultural event. Witness red carpet premieres, attend film screenings, and immerse yourself in the world of cinema.

9. Opéra de Nice (Nice): For a more polished evening, enjoy a performance at the Opéra de Nice. The historic theatre features a mix of opera, ballet, and classical music performances throughout the year.

FOODS

Seafood Extravaganza

1. Bouillabaisse in Marseille:

Bouillabaisse is the crown gem of Provençal seafood cuisine. Originating from the ancient port of Marseille, this substantial fish stew is a symphony of aromas. Fresh catches, including kinds like sea bass, mullet, and monkfish, are cooked with aromatic herbs, saffron, and tomatoes, producing a delicious broth. Served with a side of rouille (garlic mayonnaise) and crusty bread, it's a typical flavor of the Mediterranean.

2. Pissaladière in Nice:

This renowned Nicoise delicacy is a savory tart cooked with a foundation of caramelized onions, anchovies, and olives, all topped upon a flaky pastry crust. The outcome is a balanced combination of sweet, salty, and briny tastes that embodies the spirit of Provençal cuisine.

Wine and Tastings

3. Côte de Provence Vineyards:

The vineyards of the Côte de Provence are a tribute to the region's rich viti cultural legacy. Embark on a wine tour and experience the magnificent estates located between rolling hills and vine covered landscapes. Sample a broad choice of wines, including the outstanding rosés for which the area is known. Learn about the rigorous winemaking process, and taste the unique terroir conveyed in every sip.

4. Châteauneuf du Pape:

Venture into the nearby Rhône Valley to find the famed vines of Châteauneuf du Pape. Here, you'll meet strong reds, recognized for their rich tastes and deep character and climate, creates wines that are treasured by aficionados worldwide.

Local Markets and Gourmet Shops

5. Forville Market in Cannes:

A sensory feast awaits at the Forville Market in Cannes. Wander among vendors loaded with colorful fruit, fragrant spices, and handmade cheeses. Engage with local sellers who are enthusiastic about sharing their culinary delights

6. Gourmet Shops in Aix-en-Provence:

Explore the alleys of Aix-en-Provence and find gourmet stores that exhibit the region's culinary brilliance. From boutique olive oil makers to artisanal chocolatiers, these enterprises offer a selection of unique treats. Sample local delights like calissons, a classic almond dessert, or browse among varieties of truffles and artisan cheeses.

SHOPPING SPREE

Fashion Boutiques

1. Avenue des Champs-Élysées (Cannes):

Avenue des Champs-Élysées in Cannes is a dream for fashion fans. This elegant strip is studded with designer boutiques and luxury stores, where you can discover the newest designs from famous fashion labels. From haute couture to stylish accessories, the items here are a reflection of the Riviera's reputation for flair and refinement.

2. Rue d'Antibes (Cannes):

Rue d'Antibes, next to the Croisette, is another lively retail center in Cannes. This boulevard is home to a mix of high end apparel stores, fashionable businesses, and attractive cafés. It's the ideal spot to examine the newest fashion trends and find unique things that encapsulate the spirit of the Riviera's stylish lifestyle.

Artisanal Markets

3. Marché Forville (Cannes):

For a sample of local delicacies and handcrafted crafts, visit Marché Forville in Cannes. This bustling market is a sensory feast, with kiosks loaded with fresh fruit, aromatic spices, and artisan crafts. Engage with local sellers and discover distinctive Provençal items, from olive oils to handcrafted crafts. It's an opportunity to immerse yourself in the true charm of the place.

4. Cours Saleya (Nice):

Cours Saleya in Nice is a busy marketplace that accommodates an assortment of markets throughout the week. On some days, you'll find a lively flower market, while on others, it morphs into a colorful food market.
The booths brim with bright blossoms, local vegetables, and handcrafted crafts. It's a chance to enjoy the colorful ambiance of a Provençal market while indulging in some delicious shopping.

Antique Treasures

5. Carré d'Or Antiques District (Nice):

For enthusiasts of antique treasures, the Carré d'Or neighborhood in Nice is a paradise of vintage antiquities. Explore the quaint streets, where antique stores and galleries present a selection of timeless treasures. From gorgeous furniture to stunning artwork, each piece conveys a narrative of history and skill. Ifyou're a seasoned collector, merely seeking a unique keepsake, this region provides a variety of alternatives.

6. Village of Biot:

The town of Biot, tucked in the hills above the Riviera, is famed for its handcrafted glasswork. Explore the stores and studios where expert glassblowers produce stunning masterpieces. From tiny vases and detailed sculptures, these items are both aesthetic and useful, making them beloved additions to any collection.

The French Riviera's retail culture appeals to a varied spectrum of preferences, from haute couture enthusiasts to fans of artisanal workmanship and antique treasures.

PRACTICAL TIPS FOR A SMOOTH VISIT

Local Etiquette

1. Greetings: When meeting someone, a common French greeting is a kiss on both cheeks. However, in more official contexts or with strangers, a simple handshake is fine.

2. Dress Code: Dressing cleanly and gracefully is prized on the French Riviera. In upmarket restaurants and clubs, it's important to dress properly. Beachwear is good for the beach but should be covered up while leaving the beach area.

3. Dining Etiquette: While dining, it's regarded as courteous to keep your hands on the table, and wrists resting on the edge. Wait until the host or hostess begins the dinner before you begin eating.

4. Punctuality: Being on time for appointments and reservations is highly praised. Arriving fashionably late is often not appreciated.

5. Language: While many people know English, attempting to speak basic French phrases is welcomed. A simple "Bonjour" (good morning) or "Merci" (thank you) goes a long way.

Tipping Customs

1. Restaurants: A service fee is normally included in the bill, but it's traditional to leave some modest change as an extra tip, particularly if you experienced great treatment. About 510% is common.

2. Cafes: In cafes, it's typical to round up the amount or leave tiny change as a tip.

3. Taxis: Tipping taxi drivers is usual but not mandatory. You may round up the fare or leave a modest extra amount.

4. Tour Guides: For guided tours, it's usual to tip your guide if you are happy with the service. The quantity might vary, but roughly 10% of the trip fee is a decent guideline.

Sustainable Travel Practices

1. Use Public transit: The French Riviera boasts an effective public transit system, including buses and trains. Opt for public transportation to lessen your carbon impact.

2. Support Local: Shop at local markets and eat at locally owned restaurants to support the local economy and lessen the environmental effects of chain enterprises.

3. Conserve Water: The Mediterranean environment may be dry, so be aware of water consumption. Consider reusing towels in hotels and save water while bathing or brushing your teeth.

4. Reduce Plastic Use: The Riviera's natural beauty may be tarnished by plastic garbage. Carry a reusable water bottle and shopping bag to limit plastic usage.

5. Respect Nature: When exploring the region's natural beauties, use established routes and avoid harming animals or flora. Leave no trace and dispose of rubbish correctly.

6. Choose Sustainable Accommodation: Look for ecofriendly hotels or lodgings that have implemented sustainable measures, such as recycling and energy conservation.

By following these local etiquette recommendations, tipping traditions, and sustainable travel practices, you may not only enjoy your vacation to the French Riviera but also help the preservation of its culture and environment. Enjoy your travel responsibly!

DAY TRIPS & EXCURSIONS

Discovering Nearby Towns

1. Eze Village:

Perched high above the Mediterranean, Eze Village is a lovely medieval hamlet that has tiny cobblestone alleys, quaint artisan shops, and spectacular panoramic vistas. Visit the Jardin Exotique for a beautiful botanical garden experience, and tour the remains of the Eze Castle for an insight into the town's past.

2. Saint-Paul de-Vence:

Known as the "City of Art," Saint-Paul-de Vence is a refuge for artists and art aficionados. The village is studded with galleries, workshops, and lovely stores. Wander around the small alleyways, see the artwork, and absorb the ambiance of this wonderfully preserved medieval hamlet.

3 . Châteauneuf du Pape:

Venture into the nearby Rhône Valley to find the famed vines of Châteauneuf du Pape. Here, you'll meet strong reds, recognized for their rich tastes and deep character. Immerse yourself in the rich history of winemaking and delight in tastings at some of the most recognized estates.

Scenic Drives around the Coast

5. Corniche Roads:

Take a leisurely drive along the Corniche roads, which provide spectacular views of the Mediterranean shoreline. The Corniche Moyenne, Corniche Inférieure, and Corniche Supérieure each present a distinct view of the Riviera's natural beauty. Stop at authorized spots to snap stunning images of the blue water and rocky rocks.

6. Route de la Corniche d'Or:

This gorgeous coastal route spans between Cannes and Saint-Raphaël, affording stunning views of the Esterel Massif's red cliffs contrasting against the deep blue of the Mediterranean. Numerous pullouts enable you to halt and completely admire the aweinspiring surroundings.

These day tours and excursions provide a varied variety of activities, from touring ancient cities to relishing the greatest wines and delighting in the seaside beauties. Each site encourages you to dig into the particular beauty and fascination of the French Riviera. Enjoy your experiences!

BONUS

French Riviera Phrases And Their Meanings

1. Bonjour Hello
2. Bonsoir Good evening
3. Bonne nuit Good night
4. Merci Thank you
5. De rien You're welcome
6. Excusezmoi Excuse me
7. S'il vous plaît Please
8. Oui Yes
9. Non No
10. Peutêtre Maybe
11. Parlezvous anglais ? Do you speak English?
12. Je ne parle pas bien français I don't speak French very well
13. Pouvezvous m'aider ? Can you help me?
14. Où est... ? Where is...?
15. Combien ça coûte ? How much does it cost?
16. L'addition, s'il vous plaît The bill, please
17. Je voudrais... I would like...
18. Avezvous... ? Do you have...?
19. L'eau Water
20. Le menu The menu
21. La carte The map
22. L'hôtel The hotel
23. La plage The beach
24. Le musée The museum
25. Le train The train
26. L'aéroport The airport
27. La gare The train station
28. L'office de tourisme The tourist office

29. Pouvezvous répéter, s'il vous plaît ? Can you repeat, please?
30. Je voudrais un café, s'il vous plaît I would like a coffee, please
31. L'addition, s'il vous plaît The bill, please
32. Où sont les toilettes ? Where are the toilets?
33. Je suis perdu(e) I am lost
34. Pouvezvous me recommander un restaurant ? Can you recommend a restaurant?
35. Estce que je peux payer par carte de crédit ? Can I pay by credit card?
36. À quelle heure est le dernier train pour… ? What time is the last train to…?
37. Je voudrais réserver une chambre I would like to book a room
38. Avezvous une table pour deux, s'il vous plaît ? Do you have a table for two, please?
39. Quel est le plat du jour ? What is the dish of the day?
40. Pouvezvous me donner l'heure ? Can you tell me the time?
41. Où puisje trouver un distributeur de billets ? Where can I find an ATM?
42. Je voudrais essayer ceci I would like to try this
43. Je ne mange pas de… I don't eat…
44. Avezvous un plan de la ville ? Do you have a city map?
45. Quel est le moyen de transport le plus rapide pour aller à… ? What is the fastest way to get to…?
46. Je voudrais un billet pour… I would like a ticket to…
47. Pouvezvous m'indiquer le chemin vers… ? Can you show me the way to…?

48. Où puisje acheter des souvenirs ? Where can I buy souvenirs?

49. Quelle est la météo aujourd'hui ? What is the weather like today?

50. Où puisje trouver un taxi ? Where can I find a taxi?

4 Days Itinerary

Day 1: Exploring Nice

Morning: 9:00 AM: Start your day with a leisurely breakfast at a nearby café. Try some fresh pastries and a café au lait.
10:00 AM: Visit the Promenade des Anglais. Take a leisurely walk along the famed oceanfront promenade, admiring the breathtaking views of the Mediterranean Sea.

Midday: 12:30 PM: Head to Old Town (Vieux Nice). Explore the small alleyways, and colorful marketplaces, and explore the Cathédrale Sainte-Réparate.
2:00 PM: Have lunch at a neighborhood café. Try some Nicoise delicacies like Salade Niçoise or Socca.

Afternoon: 3:30 PM: Visit the Marc Chagall National Museum to appreciate the artist's beautiful collection of paintings.
5:00 PM: Relax at the beach. Choose a location along the Promenade des Anglais and enjoy the sun and sea.

Evening: 7:30 PM: Dinner at a beachfront restaurant. Enjoy excellent seafood while viewing the sunset.
9:00 PM: Take a leisurely evening walk along the promenade. Enjoy the bustling environment and maybe even see a street act.

Day 2: Day Trip to Eze and Monaco

Morning: 9:00 AM: Depart for the historic town of Eze. Explore the cobblestone alleys and explore the Exotic Garden for panoramic views.

Midday: 12:30 PM: Have lunch in Eze. Many eateries provide spectacular views of the shore.

Afternoon: 2:30 PM: Drive or take a bus to Monaco. Visit the Prince's Palace and the Oceanographic Museum.

Evening: 7:00 PM: Explore the Casino Square and the surrounding region. Enjoy the upscale stores and maybe even try your luck at the casino.

Day 3: Antibes and Cannes

Morning: 9:00 AM: Start your day in Antibes. Visit the ancient old town, the Picasso Museum, and take a walk around the city walls.

Midday: 12:30 PM: Have lunch in Antibes. Try some local Provençal food.

Afternoon: 2:30 PM: Drive or take a short rail journey to Cannes. Visit the beautiful Croisette and the Palais des Festivals.

Evening: 7:00 PM: Enjoy a quiet evening by the beach or at a seaside café.

Day 4: St. Tropez

Morning: 9:00 AM: Head to St. Tropez. Enjoy a lovely drive along the shore.

Midday: 12:30 PM: Explore the lovely town core of St. Tropez. Visit the Place des Lices and peruse the stores.

Afternoon: 2:30 PM: Relax at one of the wonderful beaches near St. Tropez.

Evening: 7:00 PM: Have supper at a beach restaurant. Enjoy the bustling nightlife in the town.

Remember to change the route depending on your preferences and the opening hours of attractions. Enjoy your journey to the gorgeous French Riviera!

CONCLUSION

Dear Reader,

As you go on this trip through the pages of this book, I hope you've felt the draw of the French Riviera and experienced the frenetic pulse of its towns and the serene embrace of its shoreline. This guide was developed with you in mind, to be your constant companion while you explore this paradise.

Now, it's your time. Take those walks down the Promenade des Anglais in Nice, immerse yourself in the lovely alleys of Antibes, and experience the pulse of luxury in Monaco. Let the beauty of Eze and the glitz of Cannes grab your heart, and let the charm of St. Tropez leave an unforgettable impact.

Your experiences matter, and I want you to share them. Leave a review, and let others know how this guide enhanced your experience. Your thoughts have the ability to inspire other travelers on their own trips.

As you prepare for your visit, may your route be easy, and every moment be filled with wonder and discovery. May the sun kiss your skin and the Mediterranean air whisper its secrets to you. Have a safe, enriching, and wonderful journey.

Bon journey!

Printed in Great Britain
by Amazon